ideals ®
THANKSGIVING

The little farmhouse is waiting
Beneath the maples' rich yellow;
Corn shocks stand with pumpkins near,
And frost-nipped apples are mellow.

The red barn is filled with grain,
Cellar shelves hold treasures;
Oh, I am thankful to be living,
To share in autumn's pleasures!

Earle J. Grant

ISBN 0-8249-1065-6

Publisher, Patricia A. Pingry
Executive Editor, Peggy Schaefer
Art Director, Patrick McRae
Production Manager, Jan Johnson
Associate Editor, Joan Anderson
Editorial Assistant, Kathleen Gilbert
Copy Editor, Becky Maginn

Front and back covers from H. Armstrong Roberts, Inc.

Inside front cover from H. Armstrong Roberts, Inc.
Inside back cover by Ed Cooper

IDEALS—Vol. 45, No. 7 November MCMLXXXVIII IDEALS (ISSN 0019-137X) is published eight times a year,
February, March, May, June, August, September, November, December
by IDEALS PUBLISHING CORPORATION, Nelson Place at Elm Hill Pike, Nashville, Tenn. 37214
Second class postage paid at Nashville, Tennessee, and additional mailing offices.
Copyright © MCMLXXXVIII by IDEALS PUBLISHING CORPORATION.
POSTMASTER: Send address changes to Ideals, Post Office Box 148000, Nashville, Tenn. 37214-8000
All rights reserved. Title IDEALS registered U.S. Patent Office.

SINGLE ISSUE—$3.95
ONE-YEAR SUBSCRIPTION—eight consecutive issues as published—$17.95
TWO-YEAR SUBSCRIPTION—sixteen consecutive issues as published—$31.95
Outside U.S.A., add $6.00 per subscription year for postage and handling.

O Come, Let Us Sing

O come, let us sing unto the Lord:
Let us make a joyful noise to the rock of our salvation.
Let us come before his presence with thanksgiving,
And make a joyful noise unto him with psalms.
For the Lord is a great God,
And a great King above all gods.
In his hands are the deep places of the earth:
The strength of the hills is his also.
The sea is his, and he made it:
And his hands formed the dry land.
O come, let us worship and bow down:
Let us kneel before the Lord our maker.
For he is our God;
And we are the people of his pasture,
And the sheep of his hand.

Psalm 95, KJV

Photo Opposite
BREISKAR TINDEN MOUNTAINS
NORWAY
M. Thonig
H. Armstrong Roberts, Inc.

Photo Overleaf
NEWFANE, VERMONT
Fred M. Dole Productions

Month of Gold

Georgia B. Adams

There's a ting-a-linging feeling
In the air this golden day,
And the month is glad November
As the sunbeams softly play.

There's a sky that's strewn with cloud puffs,
There are wild geese flying high;
I can hear their distant honking
As I sigh an autumn sigh.

Leaves are changing colorations,
Gold and red for shades of green;
And the mountainsides are lovelier
Than I have ever seen.

All the corn is shocked and standing
In the fields, mute and at ease;
Morning frost is lying queenly;
I think everyone agrees

That this month of gold November
Holds a very special charm,
As we sprightly walk its pathways
Leaning on glad Autumn's arm.

Leaves

Sarah Louise Morris

Look at them, list to them, murmuring leaves
Tossing in sunshine, high o'er the eaves,
Curtaining gray branches, lichened and old,
With sumptuous drapings of green and gold,
Fashioned so deftly, so multiform,
Flexile of stem, defying the storm.
In her wondrous loom wise Nature weaves
Nothing more beautiful than the leaves.

Tenderly sheltering embryo flowers,
Lest winds breathe chill, and fierce the showers;
Skillfully thatching the minstrel's roof
Who builds in the woodland, far aloof
From hands marauding, his nestling's home;
Catching the song of breezes that roam,
And echoing them softly, gleefully, till
All the green hostel is with them athrill—
Great is the gladness my soul receives
From your whispered music, beautiful leaves.

List ye the wind, how it querulous grieves,
When Autumn pilfers the beautiful leaves;
Mute are the birds, and the sad skies weep,
As through the valley, o'er the hilltop steep,
She wantonly wanders, and scattereth
Their glorious beauty unto death.

Photo Opposite
CANOES
Griebeling/Miller
H. Armstrong Roberts, Inc.

Reflections

Clinton B. Price

Atop the dam, the road;
Beneath, the chuckling water
    escaping confinement;
Back of it, the pond,
Red maples, dark evergreens, yellow birch
    along its banks,
All reflected in shape and color
On the quiet, sunlit water—
Until a fish jumps,
Sending quickly widening circles
    across its surface;
Then, still water again,
With autumn foliage in full possession
    of nature's looking glass.

Photo Opposite
FALL POND
Dave Conley
The Stock Solution

Photo Overleaf
NEW ENGLAND CHURCH
Tom Grill
Comstock

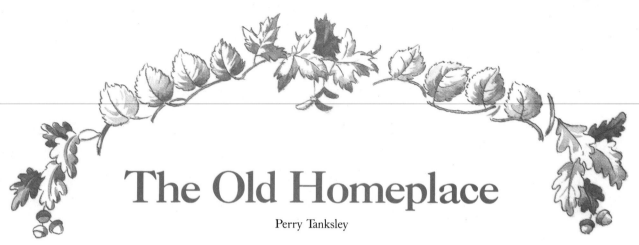

The Old Homeplace

Perry Tanksley

I've got to turn aside
From life's exhausting pace
And make a pilgrimage
Back to the old homeplace.

Familiar childhood paths
Through shady woods I'll roam,
And I at last shall stand
Upon the hills of home.

And there forgotten dreams,
Ideals that slipped away,
Will all come marching back
When I go home today.

And I, refreshed, shall then
Turn back to life's mad race,
If only I today
Can see the old homeplace.

We Offer Thanks

Stella Craft Tremble

Now in the strife and tenseness of this hour,
Acknowledging His love that stilled the sea,
We turn with thankful hearts to higher power,
Who overthrows all hate and enmity.

Another year the arm of liberty,
Outstretched to hold us safe from bomb or plane,
Has held secure from peril and disaster
America—our home and proud domain.

As autumn ends with bursting bins of grain
And gleaner stores his harvest plow away,
We offer thanks for fertile prairie land
And humbly pause in gratitude to pray.

The beauty of our country we have known,
Its forests, rivers, plains, its hills and seas;
Awareness of our heritage we own,
Traditions, Constitution—all of these.

But let us pray and ever watchful be
That our great country stay forever free!

Photo Opposite
OLD IRONSIDES
Jeff Gnass Photography, Inc.

First Letter Home

Pamela Kennedy

Dearest Mother,

I don't know when this letter will reach the shores of England, but I want to set down the account of our voyage now while all the experiences are fresh in my mind.

Our leave-taking lasted much longer than expected due to ill winds and leaky ships. We had hoped to sail with the *Speedwell,* a sister ship, but she proved unseaworthy and had to be left in England. Unfortunately, by the time the weeks of delays had passed, we had eaten all the foodstuffs we had set aside for the voyage and were starting on those provisions meant for the setting up of our new home. In addition, we were now beginning the voyage in September instead of the early summer, and the seas appeared as angry as we over the delay.

When we finally did depart the shores of home, we were 102 passengers (thirty-four of them children), and none of us were used to the pitching seas and dankness of the ship's cramped quarters. It seemed that all were sick a goodly amount of the first weeks, and the moaning and the stench were hard to bear.

My pregnancy added to my personal discomfort, and our three children battled boredom, illness, and one another. The ship's crew, unaccustomed to their cargo of Pilgrims, treated us, for the most part, as a nuisance. It seemed our fervor displeased them most, and each time we assembled for morning prayers the seamen gathered to taunt us with vulgar profanities, insults, and bawdy oaths, and one young man, in particular, was most offensive. We had hoped to win the seamen's respect by piety, but quite another thing transpired. The young man of whom I write was taken one day with a strange and sudden ailment. Cursing violently to the end, he died within a day. So superstitious were his fellows that they took his demise as indication of God's disfavor and, from then on, allowed our worship times to continue unimpeded.

As I mentioned before, our food supplies were sadly lacking from the first, and once we regained our appetites there was precious little to eat. Salt or pickled beef, pork and fish, dried ground peas, and a little Holland cheese were our staples. Round, hard wheat biscuits gave us bulk, but after a few weeks these became as hard as cannonballs and had to be beaten into pieces with a mallet. Oh, what we would have given for some of your good, hot pudding or a savory stew, dear Mother!

Elder Brewster has been most appreciated for setting up school for the children. Having brought over 200 books, he shares with all who can read. The children learn their letters from the family bibles, and on ship the lessons helped to pass the time. The older boys were under the instruction of the younger men, such as John Alden, enjoying the exercise of wrestling matches and such sport as space allowed. For the most, however, the days on ship were long and bone-chilling; we were continually knocked about below decks, wondering if the ship would survive.

We had hoped to stay to a southerly route, but storms and currents conspired against us, and the *Mayflower* carried us north. There, I fear to tell you, we all were sure we had met our deaths. In a storm unlike any I have ever seen, or even dreamed was possible, our little ship was tossed and torn. Freezing water poured through the decks to our quarters below, drenching tiny ones and old alike. With a thunderous crack, the main beam amidship split and buckled. The deck splintered, the water poured in upon us, and the men gathered helplessly, wondering what to do to save the ship. Again the Providence of God prevailed as someone recalled the great Iron Screw we had brought from Holland to help in raising houses in the New World. Set to the beam, it raised the broken place enough to provide us with some security.

More than once, I must admit, we discussed the possibility of heading back and abandoning our venture; but after much discussion and prayer, Elder Bradford determined, "We must commit ourselves to the will of God and resolve to proceed."

Despite the terrible seas, the unrelenting darkness, the freezing cold, and the abominable stench, time continued, and so it was I came to the time of birthing. I had so hoped to be on firm ground in a warm house in the New World when the baby came, but it was not to be. There, in the Great Cabin, carried on the very breast of the sea, I labored and brought forth a

veritable son of Neptune! We named him Oceanus and he seemed for all on board to be an omen of better times to come.

But immediately after the birth of tiny Oceanus, our people began to contract the dreaded scurvy. Despite our prayers, young William Butten died and was buried at sea. Others showed the telltale signs— swollen limbs, chills, and fevers. We despaired for them and continued imploring God to hasten us to land.

Then, at last, on November 9 at seven in the morning, we heard the blessed sound, "LAND! LAND HO!" Sixty-five days our voyage had lasted, and we rushed on deck to assure ourselves that the call was true. There before us lay the long, low stretch of brown and gray. It was unknown, a mystery of undiscovered sights and sounds, but it was our hope. Stephen, the children, and I joined the others as we fell to our knees with tears of joy and relief, and Elder Brewster led us in the singing of Psalm 100.

As I write this now I do not know what the future holds, but I do know that for us there is a future. We give thanks to God for safe passage and trust His good help to guard us all. What joy to know my little Oceanus will be a citizen of this new land, and together we shall all strive to make of it what we can.

You are constantly in my thoughts; please pray for us, dear Mother.

Your devoted daughter,

Elizabeth Hopkins

Elizabeth Hopkins

Gypsy Wind

Starrlette L. Howard

A Gypsy wind blew in today.
Her painted skirt, so bright and bold,
Swirled round and round her as she danced;
The leaves swirled red and orange and gold.
Then at night, in full moon bright,
She carried in her crystal ball
To sprinkle the ground with a glimmering white
As she whispered a fond farewell to fall.

Untamed Beauty

Letitia Morse Nash

Now comes Autumn, gayly flaunting
All her skirts of flaming hue;
Orange, purple, red, and golden,
Somber brown, and steely blue.

Tresses dark as midnight, glowing
With the jewels of the fall;
Purple grapes and leaves of yellow,
Sunlight glinting over all.

Twinkling feet that dance so lightly
Stirring piles of fallen leaves,
Sounds of song or windy laughter—
Glorious Autumn is proud and free.

In her arms outstretched before her,
Golden grain, and fruit, and flower
Bring us joyousness and plenty,
Gifts to fill each happy hour.

Oh, the wealth of Autumn's splendor,
How we love her wild, sweet ways;
And we cherish all her beauties
Through the happy, carefree days.

COLLECTOR'S CORNER

A variety of collectible clocks

To have an old clock or a collection of them in your home is a multi-sensory experience. The swinging pendulums and sweeping hands of clocks delight the eye. The friendly sounds of ticking and bells and chimes are music to the ears. The feel of polished old wood and brass brings pleasure to the hands.

The special affection people have for their clocks is apparent in this note found inside an antique grandfather clock: "You are a friend to all of us, a regulator on the speed of our lives, and a faithful link between a generation gone and a generation yet to come." People who ac-

quire clocks as heirlooms often see themselves as caretakers rather than owners of them, since they plan to pass the clocks on to the next generation.

Many clock collectors are attracted to the hobby because they enjoy unraveling the threads of history. They want to know where a clock originated, who made it, and what style and period it represents.

The personality of a clock gains an added dimension if you know who used the clock and how it affected the people who used it. For example, one clock collection contains a nineteenth-century regulator clock that was used to signal the opening and closing of the old Philadelphia stock exchange. A turn-of-the-century advertising clock in the same collection heralds Calumet Baking Powder. A third clock is an early twentieth-century time clock that served scores of working people every day for several decades.

People also collect clocks because they appreciate the appearance of them. In fact, European nobility and royal patrons of the arts, during the sixteenth century and later, collected clocks primarily for aesthetic appeal. The royal courts commissioned some of the greatest artists of the time to make clocks that

Ansonia iron case mantel clock, circa 1902

Photos courtesy of The Watch and Clock Museum

Boston-style banjo clock, circa 1820

Eight-day ogee shelf clock movement, circa 1837

Seth Thomas thirty-hour ogee shelf clock, circa 1850

are characterized by extravagant appearance and ornate design. The clocks were more important as objects of curiosity and prestige than they were as timekeepers.

Today, clock collecting has grown into a hobby for people from all walks of life. The vast spectrum of collectible American clocks ranges from the banjo clock, the first uniquely American case design, to the Mickey Mouse alarm clock. While early American grandfather clocks with handcrafted wooden cases are increasingly rare and beyond the means of many collectors, mantel, shelf, and wall clocks have survived because they were mass-produced and were durable. The result of Yankee ingenuity, some of these clocks feature attractive veneers, hand-painted dials, and reverse paintings on glass.

For the mechanically inclined, collecting old clocks brings great pleasure and satisfaction when, after some minor tinkering, an old clock begins to work properly once again. The mechanical works of an old clock can be elegantly simple and fairly easy to understand. Often, all that is needed to put one in operation is the gentle touch of a human hand.

Modern technology is changing both the inner and outer appearance of clocks. Digital displays are replacing traditional faces and hands. The mechanical clock—with its train of toothed wheels—has been made obsolete by quartz technology. Collecting clocks has become extremely popular because people want to preserve a tradition of clockmaking that seems to be vanishing. The growth of the hobby is reflected in the membership of the National Association of Watch and Clock Collectors, an organization founded in 1943 which has over 30,000 members today.

A clock captivates people because it is more than just a functional device used to order our lives. To some, a clock is a piece of history; to others it is a piece of furniture or a work of art; and to still others it is a mechanical challenge. Even one clock, for the right person, may be all these things.

Jed Kensinger

Ocean Mood

Anonymous

The sea crashed over the grim gray rocks,
  It thundered beneath the height,
It swept by reef and sandy dune,
It glittered beneath the harvest moon
  That bathed it in yellow light.

Shell and seaweed and sparkling stone
  It flung on the golden sand,
Strange relics torn from its deepest caves—
Sad trophies of wild, victorious waves—
  It scattered upon the strand.

Spars that looked so strong and true
  When the gallant ship was launched,
Shattered and broken, and flung to the shore,
While the tide in its deep, triumphant roar,
  Rang the dirge for old wounds long stanched.

Pretty trifles that it had brought
   From many a foreign clime,
Snatched by the storm from the clinging clasp
Of hands that the lonely will never grasp,
   While the world yet counteth time.

Back, back to its depths went the ebbing tide,
   Leaving its stores to rest
Unsought and unseen in the silent bay,
To be gathered again, ere close of day,
   To the ocean's mighty breast.

As Winter Approaches

As winter steadily approaches,
The animals and I
Engage in like activities
'Neath a dark November sky.

We scurry about compulsively,
Making nests snug and tight,
Blocking out the arctic wind's
Ferociously chilling bite.

We gather together provisions now—
Food for the months ahead;
I carry in wood for a roaring fire,
While they seek leaves for beds.

I whisper a prayer as, patiently,
I await the impending storm,
That God will keep all of his creatures
    safe
And blessedly fed and warm.

Peggy Mlcuch
Cambridge, VT

Grandma's Feather Bed

There was a special night
That time does not erase;
I lay in Grandma's feather bed
By the crackling fireplace.

Grandma slept beside me,
Her hair pinned in a fold;
The house smelled sweet of apple tarts,
Cooked on the black wood stove.

Morning came so quickly,
It really seemed too soon;
Grandma eased out of the bed
And tiptoed from the room.

The fire slowly dwindled,
Glowing soft and red;
I snuggled just a little more
In Grandma's feather bed.

Evelyn Steen Taylor
Monroe, LA

Editor's Note: Readers are invited to submit unpublished, original poetry, short anecdotes, and humorous reflections on life for possible publication in future I*deals* issues. Please send copies only; manuscripts will not be returned. Writers will receive $10 for each published submission. Send materials to "Readers' Reflections," Ideals Publishing Corporation, Nelson Place at Elm Hill Pike, Nashville, Tennessee 37214.

Reflections

Aging Autumn

She wore sparkling gypsy earrings,
Mantilla of gold lace,
And sweeping gown of amethyst;
I could not see her face.

Strolling down our sunlit street,
She flirted with her fan;
Maple trees blushed tangerine,
And the fall began.

This morning in my garden, *look*!
She does not stir at all,
Bowed in silent resignation
Beneath a silver shawl.

Z. Vilet Bennett
Joplin, MO

Grateful Praise

A startled pheasant whirs aloft on brilliant wings
Displaying, to our joy, the art and skill of God.
Beyond the river's chilly breath the church bell rings;
Our hearing hearts in silent glad amen applaud.

Forsake the window now; doff aprons. Time to go.
Collect the boisterous, fresh-dressed youngsters; halt their pranks.
Leave fragrant loaves and pies, the turkey roasting low,
To celebrate with friends through prayers and hymns of thanks.

Juanita Y. Holter
Santa Barbara, CA

November's Moods

I love November's quiet moods,
Her wan and weeping solitude,
Her taciturn, unsmiling sky,
Her lonely winds that whistle by,
The calm submission of her leas,
The resignation of her trees.

I love her undemanding days,
Her patient, pious, peaceful ways,
Her monochrome and modest gown,
Her solid sense in settling down
Before the winter's wrath intrudes.
I love November's quiet moods.

Ruth Van Gorder
Lake Ariel, PA

The Pilgrims Give Thanks

Marjorie Lindsey Brewer

Just look upon the land and see the yield
Of pumpkins, corn, and squash in every field.
The shocks of corn are glistening in the sun
With coats of frost on every one.

Come, let us have a feast with praise
To God, who blessed the crops we raise.
Have Massasoit and all his men
Bring deer and visit us again.

Together, we will roast the meat—
Wild turkey, venison we'll eat.
Some pumpkins, corn, and hoe-cake bread
Will grace the board when thanks are said.

At last, we have our feast prepared.
We thank our God for how we've fared,
For crops that He has helped us grow
And for the seed we have to sow.

Our Horn of Plenty overflows
With products from the land we chose.
We give our thanks to God above
For all His care and help and love.

Thanksgiving

Virginia Katherine Oliver

Humbly before God
And proudly before man,
We give thanks.

Thanksgiving is a time for remembering,
And what memories are ours!
We, who dwell in a land
Where freedom prevails
And where honor and righteousness are
    our code,
Remember the solid foundation
Upon which our nation is built.

As a people we stand united
In an effort to preserve that which is our
    heritage.
For the opportunities and privileges
Which have benefited us as individuals
And as a nation,
And for the blessings
Which have been bestowed upon us,
We are grateful.

In our hearts we give thanks
That we can say to all the world,
"I am an American!"

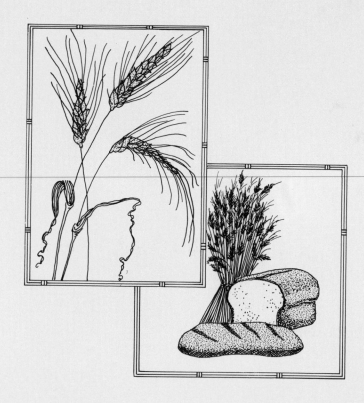

The Feast Time of the Year

Anonymous

This is the feast time of the year,
When Plenty pours her wine of cheer,
And even humble boards may spare
To poorer poor a kindly share.

While bursting barns and granaries know
A richer, fuller overflow,
And they who dwell in golden ease
Bless without toil, yet toil to please.

This is the feast time of the year,
The blessed Advent draweth near;
Let rich and poor together break
The bread of love for Christ's sweet sake,

Against the time when rich and poor
Must ope for Him a common door
Who comes a guest, yet makes a feast,
And bids the greatest and the least.

After the Storm

Stella Flowers Hastings

The earth smells dank and new and clean;
Upon the grass so freshly green,
The fallen leaves make yellow beds.

The pepper trees with ferny boughs
Are bending low, weighed down with rain,
Drizzling, drizzling rain.
The jeweled drops on every leaf
Glint and gleam in autumn's light.

The date palms stand with arms outstretched,
Draped in fruits and leaves of green.
Holding rain in woody cups,
They lift their stately heads to God,
And drink ambrosia, sweet, divine.

The south winds blow and wave the palms,
Kiss the poppies along the path,
Then, laughing, hurry on their way.

Glimpsing rosy streaks of sun
Belting the mountain's snowy crest,
The storm maids vanish in a mist.
And yonder, south, a rainbow glows,
Proclaims o'er the sky a golden day,
And brings new hope to humankind.

ZUEHLKE

Country Lanes

Phyllis C. Michael

I'm thankful, Lord, for country lanes
That wind through autumn-dressed trees,
And for that playful little imp,
A crisp November breeze,
That sings a tune and makes the leaves
Dance in a merry way,
While busy gray squirrels hurry about
Storing nuts away.

I'm thankful, Lord, for the autumn sky,
Pink sunsets in the west,
And for this glorious time of year,
The time I love the best.
I think of summer grains now stored
In barns and in corn bins, too,
Canned tomatoes and jellies that sparkle—
A tantalizing view!

I'm thankful I see as I walk down the lane
A fence with a swinging gate,
A footworn path and a little house
Where I know my loved ones wait
All seated around a laden table,
And it makes life worth the living.
Yes, Lord, country lanes in my memory
Make a true Thanksgiving.

Tantalizing Side Dishes

Garden Harvest Casserole
Makes 6 to 8 servings

- 1 cup sliced and unpeeled eggplant
- 1 cup thinly sliced carrots
- 1 cup sliced green beans
- 1 cup diced potatoes
- 2 medium tomatoes, quartered
- 1 small yellow squash, sliced
- 1 small zucchini, sliced
- 1 medium onion, sliced
- ½ cup chopped green pepper
- ½ cup chopped cabbage
- 3 cloves garlic, crushed
- 3 sprigs parsley, chopped
  Freshly ground black pepper
- 1 cup beef bouillon
- ⅓ cup vegetable oil
- 2 teaspoons salt
- ¼ teaspoon tarragon
- ½ bay leaf, crumbled

Mix vegetables together and place into a shallow baking dish (13 x 9 x 2 inches). Sprinkle parsley and grind pepper over all. At this point you can refrigerate until ready to bake. Preheat oven to 350°. Pour bouillon into a small saucepan; add oil, salt, tarragon, and bay leaf. Heat to boiling; correct seasonings. Pour over vegetables. Cover baking dish with aluminum foil; bake 1 to 1½ hours or until vegetables are just tender and are still colorful. Carefully stir vegetables occasionally; but to preserve color, don't lift cover off for very long.

Note: You can substitute other vegetables if they are in harvest and they appeal to you.

Anise Carrots
Makes 4 to 6 servings

- 1 pound carrots, peeled and cut diagonally in ½-inch slices
- 2 tablespoons butter or margarine
- 1 teaspoon anise seed, crushed
- ¼ cup orange juice

Cook carrots in lightly salted water 10 to 12 minutes or until tender; drain. Add butter and anise seed; cook 1 minute. Stir in orange juice and heat thoroughly.

Festival Vegetables
Makes 4 to 6 servings

- ⅓ cup butter or margarine
- 1 10-ounce package frozen broccoli spears, thawed and cut in ½-inch pieces
- 1 10-ounce package frozen corn, thawed
- 3 tablespoons chopped sweet red pepper
- 1 ¼ teaspoons sweet basil, crumbled
- ½ teaspoon garlic salt
- ⅛ teaspoon crushed red pepper
- ⅛ teaspoon ground black pepper

Melt butter in large skillet. Add remaining ingredients; stir well. Simmer, covered, 8 to 10 minutes, stirring occasionally.

Yam Apple Scallop
Makes 6 to 8 servings

- ¼ cup packed brown sugar
- 2 tablespoons chopped pecans
- 1 teaspoon ground cinnamon
- ½ teaspoon ground nutmeg
- ½ teaspoon ground coriander
- 2 tablespoons sherry
- 2 tablespoons butter or margarine, melted
- 1 pound sweet potatoes, cooked or 1 pound canned sweet potatoes, drained and sliced ¼-inch thick
- 2 apples, cored, pared, and sliced ¼-inch thick
- 1 8¼-ounce can crushed pineapple, drained

Preheat oven to 350°. Combine sugar, nuts, and spices; set aside. Combine sherry and butter; set aside. Layer half each of the sweet potatoes, apples, pineapple, spice mixture, and sherry mixture in ungreased 2-quart casserole; repeat layers. Bake, covered, 30 minutes. Uncover and bake 10 to 15 minutes longer.

Pumpkin Puree

- 1 pie pumpkin, peeled and cut into small pieces (remove seeds and strings)
  Enough water to steam the vegetable

Place pumpkin pieces over boiling water in a large pot. Steam until tender. Mash or sieve, keeping pulp as dry as possible. Use immediately or cool over cold water and freeze.

Note: Winter squash can also be used.

Photo Opposite, GARDEN HARVEST CASSEROLE

Lineage

Harriet Mills McKay

They say I have Aunt Orpha's chin,
And hair the same as Mother's;
My actions are just like my dad's,
My temper like my brother's.

I'm told I have Aunt Mary's eyes,
And Great-grandmother's nose. . . .
It gives me much to think about,
And I find no repose.

My great-great-great-great-grandparents
Number sixty-four;
Another generation back
Are twice as many more.

When I began to figure up
The branches on my tree,
I found I had a forest full
Of worthy ancestry.

The thing that worries me is this:
I frequently recall
That I'm so much like ancestors
I'm not like me at all!

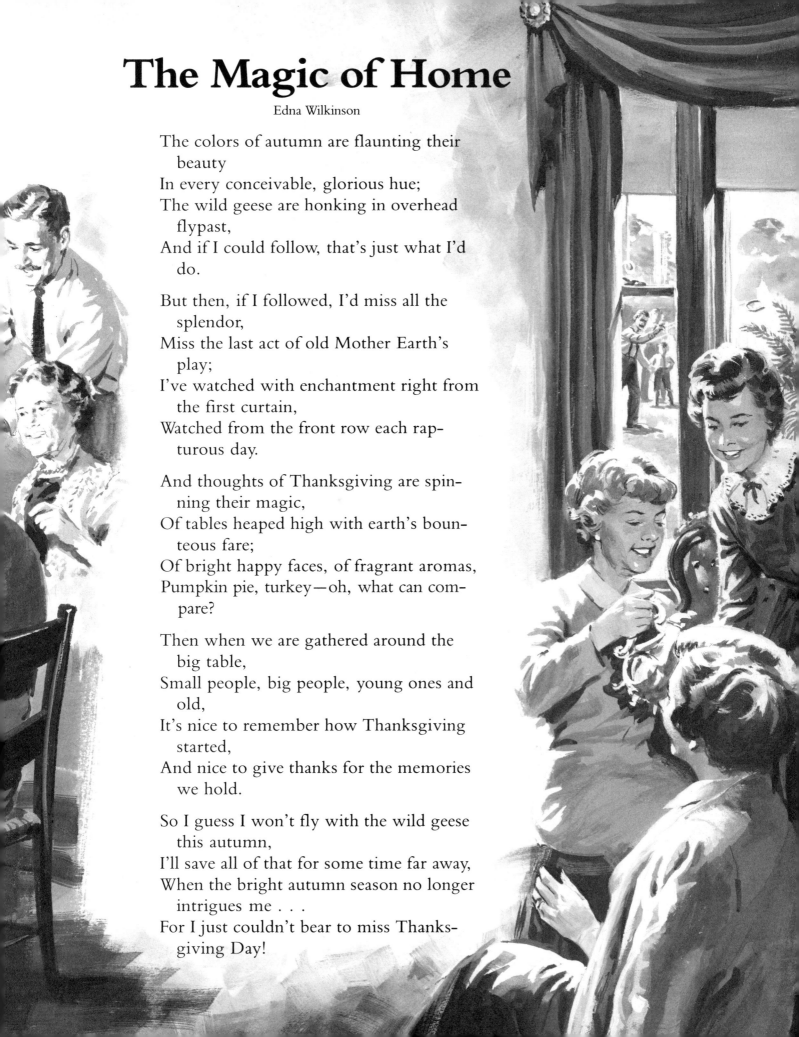

The Magic of Home

Edna Wilkinson

The colors of autumn are flaunting their
    beauty
In every conceivable, glorious hue;
The wild geese are honking in overhead
    flypast,
And if I could follow, that's just what I'd
    do.

But then, if I followed, I'd miss all the
    splendor,
Miss the last act of old Mother Earth's
    play;
I've watched with enchantment right from
    the first curtain,
Watched from the front row each rap-
    turous day.

And thoughts of Thanksgiving are spin-
    ning their magic,
Of tables heaped high with earth's boun-
    teous fare;
Of bright happy faces, of fragrant aromas,
Pumpkin pie, turkey—oh, what can com-
    pare?

Then when we are gathered around the
    big table,
Small people, big people, young ones and
    old,
It's nice to remember how Thanksgiving
    started,
And nice to give thanks for the memories
    we hold.

So I guess I won't fly with the wild geese
    this autumn,
I'll save all of that for some time far away,
When the bright autumn season no longer
    intrigues me . . .
For I just couldn't bear to miss Thanks-
    giving Day!

Our Prayer of Thanks

Kay Hoffman

We humbly bow before you, Lord,
On this Thanksgiving Day
To lift our prayers of gratitude
For all your caring ways.

As you have blessed our harvest, Lord,
Let us remember, too,
That we should share with those in need
As you would have us do.

Around this festive board today
Are those we hold most dear,
And in our midst your presence, Lord,
Seems so very near.

We're thankful for this land we love,
For sod and sky and tree,
For pilgrims who braved unknown seas
That all may worship free.

We're thankful for each blessing, Lord,
You send along our way;
But may our greater "thanks" be shown
In serving you each day.

Till Next Thanksgiving Day

Loise Pinkerton Fritz

Thanksgiving Day is over,
The table's now bereft,
The dishes have been washed and dried,
The families all have left.

The feeble hands that waved farewell
Are placed upon the laps
Of those who welcomed families home—
Dear mothers and dear dads.

Now silent is the kitchen,
Where all the bustling was,
And empty is each homey room
Which now must see some dust!

But treasured are the memories
That in each heart will stay
To keep alive the family love
Till next Thanksgiving Day.

Recollections

William Gerard Chapman

When the winds of bleak November
Down the chimney moan and sigh,
Stirring into life each ember
Till the flames roar fierce and high,
Then my thoughts revert to boyhood,
When Thanksgiving Day drew nigh.

In the flames I see the farmhouse
And the woodland brown and sere
Where the darting woodland creatures
Bolted when I drew too near;
Scenes which ever shall be cherished
In the burning logs appear.

I can see the deep old cellar
Where the apple bins, piled high,
Overshadowed heaps of pumpkins
Golden as the sunset sky,
And the casks of new fall cider
Stood along the wall close-by.

As the old-time scenes are fading
While the firelight slowly dies,
Visions of a groaning table
Are presented to my eyes,
And I almost scent the fragrance
Of the mince and pumpkin pies.

Family Love

Mary Clark Williams

Family love
Is like a strong band,
Both binding
And flexible.
It holds the generations together,
Linking the past
And the future.
It is the beginning
Of a community,
The beginning of a city,
The beginning of a nation.
As the love
For a family grows,
So grows the love
For a community,
For a city,
For a nation,
And for the world.
Families grow and expand
According to the love
Each person, in a unique way,
Contributes
To them.
There is room for each person
In the band
Of family love.

Thanksgiving Time

Elisabeth Weaver Winstead

November leaves come tumbling down
To sweep the cloud-gray sky.
And from the empty cornfield rows,
The bronze-tipped pheasants fly.

Gold pears adorn the orchard trees,
And squash reflects gold days.
Ripe apples gleam in shining bowls,
Near hearth fires all ablaze.

Large pumpkins line the roadside patch,
The barn holds fragrant hay.
We thank our God for nature's gifts,
Given to us this day.

This treasured harvest feast we share
With those we cherish best;
With happy hearts, we bow our heads
In gratitude expressed.

Canning Time

Carice Williams

It's canning time at home once more,
With countless things to do.
There are red tomatoes to be canned
And Concord grapes, so blue,
Corn as yellow as the sun,
And beets like rubies rare,
For nature has produced her best
In harvest's yield so fair.

And as I fill each jar and glass
With extra pride and care,
They glimmer in the soft sunlight
Like jewels, bright and fair.
I always like this time of year
And proudly pat myself
Each time I view this row of jars
Upon my pantry shelf.

Apple Jelly
Verna Sparks

Today I made apple jelly
Recalling a day when we
Gathered wine red apples
Beneath the apple tree.

I thought of apple cider
Our grandpa used to make;
I thought of a day when Mother
Made apple-dapple cake.

I thought of apple dumplings
And deep-dish apple pie;
I thought of apple orchards
And swallows in the sky.

I couldn't keep from thinking
While I boiled my jelly down,
Of the fragrant, old-time sweetness
Of apples all around.

Harvest Magic

Mamie Ozburn Odum

Harvest days are filled with magic,
All the earth seems ripe and round,
And the yellow rustling fodder
Sighs as cornstalks are cut down.

Every ear of corn is gathered,
Filling cribs to overflow;
Taste the tang of ripened apples
With their red skins all aglow.

Harvest days accompany autumn
With chestnuts falling fat and round,
And yellow pumpkins resting plump
Like golden balls upon the ground.

Oh, the russet and the scarlet
Dress the trees along with gold,
Their gay aprons filled with magic;
Same old story, new, yet old.

Autumn nights seem soft and dreamy,
Crickets chirping loud and free,
And the katydids a-harping,
In the weeping willow tree.

Falling leaves clap pitter-patter,
With breezy greetings when they meet,
Whirling, tumbling, nodding sweetly,
Dancing as on fairies' feet.

Harvest days are filled with magic,
The richest gifts come from the sod;
With the harvest comes Thanksgiving
As we kneel in thanks to God.

Photo Opposite
FARMERS' MARKET
FREDERICA, DELAWARE
Grant Heilman
Grant Heilman Photography, Inc.

Autumn Days

Mrs. Paul E. King

The frost lies in the meadow, and
The corn's a parchment brown;
The bright orange pumpkins wonder whether
They'll be pie or clown.

The purple grapes hang juicy ripe
'Neath leaves that once were green;
And tangled red-orange bittersweet
Along the fence is seen.

The leaves parade fall's colors bright,
All shades from red to brown;
And leaf smoke spreads a misty haze
O'er valley, hill, and town.

The chestnut popped his pretty vest
To let us peek inside
And see the goodies, brown and smooth,
Which 'neath the prickles hide.

The earth smells clean and fragrant, while
A chill breeze fills the air. . . .
I walk today with thankful heart
Midst autumn's glories rare.

My Harvest

Beulah Stoneman Douglas

I will sing you a song of the autumn:
Summer's death, winter's birth,
With cold, wet mist on the leaves,
And hoarfrost on the earth;

Of moon that through thin foliage
Lends warmth to the chilling night;
Of the haunting scent of wood smoke
Like a blue haze in moonlight;

Of wind in chaotic flurry
Shaking doors, drifting leaves,
As it whirls over hill and down dale,
Howling low around the eaves;

Of the generous harvest of summer
Against bare winter's cold,
Yellow corn and bright pumpkins
Packed safe now in the fold.

Heart, count thy blessings
That long as winter stays,
Autumn's stores may cheer us
Till springtime's brighter days.

Photo Opposite
A LANTERN'S GLOW
Bob Taylor Creative Photography

Country Chronicle

Lansing Christman

Indian summer is a warm-weather respite between first frost and hard freeze, coming in the fall, in October or November. I find it especially delightful when the gentle pause comes at Thanksgiving time, just before deep snows begin to blanket the hills.

As the year is coming to a close, Indian summer offers a pleasant counterbalance to coming winter, and it is a lingering reminder of the warm weather just behind us. Look out over a lake or pond on a November morning to see mist rising almost mystically. This is a sign of Indian summer. In the forenoon sunshine you can see a pale mist hovering above the furrow left by the plowman. And on a soft afternoon, you see a haze hovering over field and wood, suspended there like a thin cloud.

You can smell Indian summer, as well. There is the earthy odor of the freshly turned earth as

farmers ready their fields for a dormant period. You can smell the aroma of witch hazel blooms, the shucks of hickory and butternuts, the ripened leaves and frosted mints. You can sense Indian summer in the fragrance of the wild grape thickets and in the wood smoke spiraling aimlessly from a chimney top.

You can hear Indian summer in the clamor of gabbling geese winging in vee formations on their way south, piercing the skies like an arrow. Crickets chirp pensively as they while away the hours. There is the song sparrow's sweet refrain from a garden hedge.

And you can feel Indian summer in the warmth of the days, warmth which expresses a certain tranquility and gentleness in the season. You can feel Indian summer in the silken threads of gossamer strands lightly clinging to your feet as you walk through damp paths of dry grass.

Indian summer is a time to experience the richness of a fleeting, gentle season. It is a time to be thankful for the year which is passing and to look forward to the drama of the season just ahead.

Photo Overleaf
HUMBOLDT NATIONAL FOREST
NEVADA
Ed Cooper Enterprises

Autumn Treasures

Elisabeth Weaver Winstead

Country lane and sheltered glen,
Mountain road or town,
With every puff of whistling wind,
The leaves come drifting down.

Rustling through the sunlit wood,
Whirling on the highway,
Rising with a billowy breeze
Chasing down a byway.

Dressed in amber or in jade,
Crimson, brown, or gold,
Leaves are autumn's treasure-trove,
Bold jewels to behold.

Vesper Time

Ruth Linnea Erickson

I look across a land that's somber hued,
And see November in a thoughtful mood
Preparing for her rest, to bring rebirth
Of vital life from out the fertile earth.

Her work is done, for now the dusty sod
Has blown upon the opened bur and pod;
And browning to a turn, the shaken trees
Have made a sheltering coverlet of leaves.

Soon night will fall, but now at evening bell
November folds her hands, for all is well.
Within their sleep the covered seeds are living,
And now it's time for vespers and thanksgiving.

Thanksgiving Potholder

Ann Marie Braaten

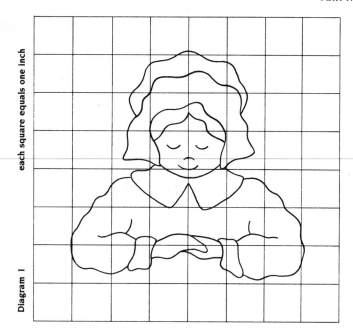

each square equals one inch

Diagram 1

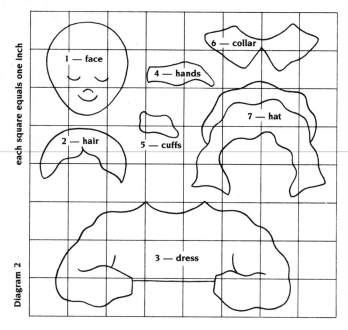

each square equals one inch

1 — face
2 — hair
3 — dress
4 — hands
5 — cuffs
6 — collar
7 — hat

Diagram 2

Materials Needed:

¼ **yard hickory-colored broadcloth**

¼ **yard 8-ounce bonded polyester batting**

Paper for cutting out patterns

⅛ **yard iron-on interfacing**

Cotton remnants:

    1 **brown print for a 3"x9" strip and a 1½"x5" strip**

    1 **dark brown print for hat (see diagram 1)**

    1 **rust print for dress**

Broadcloth remnants:

    tan for hands (2) and face

    brown for hair

    cream for cuffs (2) and collar

Matching thread

Chalk

Patterns:

Step One: Cutting Potholder Pieces

From the hickory broadcloth, cut two 9-inch squares.

From the batting, cut one 9-inch square.

Step Two: Cutting Appliqué Pieces

Use diagram 2 as a guide to make appliqué patterns from paper. Press interfacing to the wrong sides of remnants. Place and pin appliqué patterns on remnants. Cut one each for face, hair, dress, collar, and hat. Cut two each for hands and cuffs.

Construction:

Step One: Sewing Potholder

Along one 9-inch side of the 3-inch by 9-inch brown print strip, press under ½ inch. Pin the wrong side of this strip to the right side of one hickory square having raw edges even on long sides. Topstitch along the folded edge. This will be the front of the potholder.

With the 1½-inch by 5-inch brown print strip, you will form a loop. Fold along length with right sides together. Sew a ¼-inch seam along the raw edges, leaving the small ends open. Turn right side out and press. Fold in loop shape with small ends touching. Place them on the right side of the potholder front at the top. Keep all raw edges together and the looped end facing down toward the center of the hickory square. Pin.

Place front of potholder over the batting square, wrong sides together. Pin the remaining hickory square over the potholder front, right sides together. Sew a ½-inch seam around the outside edges leaving a 3-inch opening on the bottom side for turning.

Trim corners. Turn potholder to right side out. Slip-stitch opening closed.

Step Two: Appliquéing

Use chalk to draw details of dress, hat, and face on cut pieces. Beginning with piece number 1 (use diagram 1 as a positioning guide), pin piece onto potholder front. Appliqué shape with a medium zigzag stitch through all layers of cloth. (Bobbin thread should match the color of potholder back.) Do not sew facial features yet. Appliqué pieces 2 through 7 in the same way and in numerical order.

Sew facial features last with a fine zigzag stitch.

Photo Opposite
THANKSGIVING POTHOLDER
Gerald Koser

A Slice of Life

Edgar A. Guest

One day in October I was puttering about my lawn when I heard on the street the almost human screech of grinding brakes. H'm, I thought to myself, two Fords are about to kiss. I turned, expecting to see the tragedy, and was surprised to discover that sound had been produced by a single car. Then out of it began to pour the great crowd of people, which only a Ford can hold—the grandmother, the grandfather, the aunt, the uncle, the mother, and the children, and last of all, the father, who was the driver—and they arranged themselves into a group and began to admire a single tree ablaze in all the glory of the Fall.

It wasn't difficult to reconstruct what had taken place. Among them, I am sure it was the mother, was one with an eye to beauty. She had caught, through the little clear space allowed her, a flash of that scarlet foliage and had called excitedly to that father, "Stop!" I fancy he wondered what it was all about, but being dutiful he obeyed the command. And there they stood for a few minutes to admire that tree then closing its year of labor in a burst of beauty.

There was something about the incident that stayed with me. Men and women grow old and feeble, beauty deserts them and at the end of their years so far as appearances go, they are at their very worst. Save the spiritual glow which comes from lives well lived, there is little about them to admire. I thought, wouldn't it be fine if we could come to the autumn time of our lives in splendor; if we could close our careers, keeping the admiration of all who have known us. And so that day this bit was done:

I want to come to autumn with the silver in
  my hair,
And maybe have the children stop to look at
  me and stare;
I'd like to reach October free from blemish
  or from taint,
As splendid as a maple tree which artists
  love to paint.

I'd like to come to autumn, with my life
  work fully done
And look a little like a tree that's gleaming
  in the sun;

I'd like to think that I at last could come
  through care and tears
And be as fair to look upon as every elm
  appears.

But when I reach October, full contented I
  shall be
If those with whom I've walked through life
  shall still have faith in me;
Nor shall I dread the winter's frost, when
  brain and body tire,
If I have made my life a thing which others
  can admire.

The Call

A. M. Caldara

Must I let go of Autumn?
Winter, come not yet;
Let the pheasant amble,
Let the pumpkins sit
Till their orange deepens
To match the rusted sky,
Till their pulp is ripened,
Immortalized in pie.

I want still to see Autumn
On hay bales in a cart,
Exposing in an ear of corn
The stuff of Autumn's heart,
And smell the tang of laden air
From apples harvest-stored,
And look into the face of fall—
A gypsy-patterned gourd.

I want to feel the Autumn's arms
Wrap round me, in the hills;
Interpret Autumn's flighty voice
Conveyed through whippoorwills;
I want to follow Autumn's track
In thistles by the fence,
Uncover Autumn's restless soul
In sallow leaf piles, dense.

Can I not go with Autumn,
Wherever her winds blow?
Or are the whipping breezes
The same that carry snow?
My feet can't help but fidget
When a milkweed sails
Past my vagrant spirit,
Past the syrup pail.

Delay your leaving, Autumn;
If I must stay behind;
Seep in my heart and pillow it
Against the winter rind.
And may the season coming
Wipe out all trace of fall
Lest in a stranded acorn
I should hear you call.

Chrysanthemum

Oliver Wendell Holmes

Ere Advent dawns with lessening days,
While earth awaits the angels' hymn,
When bare as branching coral sways
In whistling winds each leafless limb,
When spring is but a spendthrift's dream,
And summer's wealth a wasted dower
Nor dews nor sunshine may redeem,
Then autumn coins his golden flower.

Soft was the violet's vernal hue,
Fresh was the rose's morning red,
Full-orbed the stately dahlia grew—
All gone! Their short-lived beauty shed:
The shadows, lengthening, stretch at noon,
The fields are stripped, the groves are dumb,
The frost-flowers greet the icy moon—
Still blooms the bright Chrysanthemum.

Orphan of summer, kindly sent
To cheer the waning year's decline;
Of all that pitying heaven has lent,
No fairer pledge of hope than thine.
Yes! June lies hid beneath the snow,
And winter's unborn heir shall claim
In every seed that sleeps below
A spark that kindles into flame.

Fall's Lament

June E. Knight

There's a golden cast outside,
Though sky is gray o'erhead.
Impish frost ran icy fingers
Over the nasturtium bed.

Fallen leaves glow red and gold
As brightly as when on the bough.
Chrysanthemums are still ablaze,
But pansies all are dying, now.

I look to the chrysanthemums,
Whose strength endures the early frost;
Their yellow petals smile at me,
I wonder at the heavy cost.

The wind is unpredictable
With intermittent drenching rain;
The rude outdoors pushes cold
Against my frosting windowpane.

Inside the fires of home are warm—
And though my garden has to go,
The rainbow hues give place to pine and
Flowered loveliness of snow.

New Frost

Verna Sparks

There's enchantment
   In the autumn
When the leaves
   Are bright and gay,
And the fields are
   Sweet and fragrant
With the smell
   Of fresh-mown hay.

Autumn time,
   How much to offer—
Flash and whirl
   And melody;
Simple things
   To love and cherish:
Purple aster,
   Crimson tree.

Every evening
   There's a sunset
Orange and golden
   In the west.
And the morning
   Finds frost sprinkled
On the leaves
   I love the best.

Photo
FROSTED LEAVES
Terry Seif
International Stock Photo

A Time for Settling In

Carole McCray

By the time November has arrived in our area, the Laurel Mountains of Pennsylvania, we have gotten a peek at winter; the first snow has fallen, leaving a light dusting that resembles confectioners' sugar. Sighting the first snowflake floating through a gray November sky is always a weather *happening*.

To ease ourselves into colder weather, we have already made preparations. We delight in the autumn harvest we have stored. Quart and pint jars line canning shelves: a medley of pickled beets, relishes, golden peaches, and stewed tomatoes are keeping company with homemade ketchup and tomato juice. Spicy applesauce and assorted jams and jellies have been put by, and the freezer holds blackberries, blueberries, and raspberries.

Herbal vinegars, bottled and corked, sit on the old pine cupboard's shelves. We can choose from bottles of oregano, chive, thyme, or purple basil vinegars, the prettiest of them all. I like to decorate them with a ribbon at the neck of each bottle for a charming holiday gift. And I add herbal vinegars to a favorite salad oil to enhance a garden salad.

In addition to herbal vinegars, we have also harvested and dried culinary herbs. During the summer months, we gathered herbs, then tied and hung them upside down to dry. Now they have been preserved and labeled in glass containers, covered with circles of gingham fabric for the lids, and secured with grosgrain ribbons. When a low, sullen sky brings snowflakes whirling our way, our appetites develop a zest for robust meals. That is the time for hearty stews and simmering soups, flavored with basil, thyme, savory, and oregano. We are fortunate, having either raised our own herbs or bought them fresh at country markets.

Now that the herbs are dry and the holiday season is here, I like to make bouquet garni for friends. It is easy to do and is especially welcome for the cook who delights in unique seasonings. Three herbs—bay leaf, thyme, and parsley—are dried and crumbled and placed together in a four-inch square of cheesecloth. All the edges of the cloth are brought together and secured with string. I leave a length of

string attached to my bouquet garni so it can be easily removed from the pot before the soup or stew is served.

The advancement of winter in our community means preparing food for the birds, as well. We fill our bird feeders, and the black-capped chickadees return once more. I marvel at their fortitude! When the wind blows gusts of snow, these tiny creatures will peck away at the suet and fly to the feeder in sub-zero temperatures.

The return to the hearth is natural at this time of the year, and we are ready for crackling fires in the fireplace. First, firewood is stacked near the house and covered. Enough logs for several fires are stored in the old pine woodbox on the sun porch. Soon smoke can be seen curling from chimneys, and the scent of wood smoke pervades the chilling air.

The burning of a fire on the hearth dates back to ancient times. Today, as a widely welcomed pleasure, it warms us once the chilly autumn winds blow. Naturally, a fire offers heat; and the bonus of the warm glow provides a cheerful atmosphere as we are mesmerized by the sight of dancing flames, the sound of hissing logs, and the scent of burning applewood. For all these pleasures, we arrange the kindling and strike a match.

With holidays approaching, chestnuts are readily available. We like to place a dozen or so on top of the woodburner and wait for them to split open.

For some, November can be a month of melancholy moods. But the Thanksgiving holiday arrives in November, and it lifts our spirits. We need a time of gathering and celebrating in November when a bleakness falls on the landscape. Not all November days are dark and raw; the mornings can awaken us to the surprise of azure skies and crisp days. The wet, windy days are balanced with Indian summer weather calling us to gather bittersweet bouquets, set the harvest table, and invite friends for a savory country supper. And because of our preparations, we are ready for guests.

Photo Overleaf
READING, VERMONT
Fred M. Dole Productions

Frost

Charles Lotin Hildreth

The pane is etched with wonderful tracery;
Curve interlaced with curve and line with line,
Like subtle measures of sweet harmony
Transformed to shapes of beauty crystalline.

Slim, graceful vines and tendrils, of such sort
As never grew save in some fairy world
Wind up from roots of misted silver wrought
From tulip flowers and lilies half unfurled.

Shag firs and hemlocks blend with plumy palms,
Spiked cacti spring from feathery ferns and weeds,
And sea blooms, such as rock in southern calms,
Mingle their foamy fronds with sedge and reeds.

And there are flights of birds with iris wings
That shed in midair many a brilliant plume,
And scintillating shoals of swimming things
That seem to float in clear green ocean gloom.

All these the genii of the Frost last night
Wrought through the still cold hours by charm and rune;
And now, like dreams dispelled before the light,
They float away in vapor on the noon.

November

Hartley Coleridge

The mellow year is hastening to its close;
The little birds have almost sung their last,
Their small notes twitter in the dreary blast—
That shrill-piped harbinger of early snows;

The patient beauty of the scentless rose,
Oft with the Morn's hoar crystal quaintly glassed,
Hangs, a pale mourner for the summer past,
And makes a little summer where it grows:

In the chill sunbeam of the faint bright day
The dusky waters shudder as they shine,
The russet leaves obstruct the straggling way
Of oozy brooks, which no deep banks define,
And the gaunt woods, in ragged, scant array,
Wrap their old limbs with somber ivy twine.

Ideals—Your Holiday Gift

Christmas Ideals is full of holiday joy for you with its beautiful full-color photographs, artwork, poetry, and prose—all designed with great care to bring to life the sights, sounds, and aromas of the most sacred and joyous time of the year.

The Christmas issue of *Ideals* is considered by many of our readers to be a tradition of the season as important as hanging the mistletoe and trimming the tree. Mr. Timothy Gotwols of Lebanon, Pennsylvania, writes:

> *We're an Ideals family. . . . But probably Christmas Ideals are our favorites. We have a family custom that . . . on Thanksgiving evening we sing carols, and on Friday, the day after, we get out the new Ideals and the big boxful of past Christmas issues. . . . They have given us all endless hours of reading and sharing pleasure.*

Mrs. Floyd Farmer of Grants Pass, Oregon, writes:

> *I want to congratulate you on publishing such a lovely magazine as Ideals. Without a doubt it is the finest on the market, and I find it most enjoyable.*

Thank you, Mr. Gotwols and Mrs. Farmer. We appreciate those kind words and the reassurance that we are offering our readers the highest quality of editorial excellence along with the best that each season offers us in life. This is our gift to you.

And may we suggest *Ideals* would be the perfect gift to someone you hold dear, not only at Christmas, but throughout the year.

ACKNOWLEDGMENTS

THE FEAST TIME OF THE YEAR by anonymous author from *OUR HOLIDAYS IN POETRY*, compiled by Mildred P. Harrington and Josephine H. Thomas, published by The H. W. Wilson Company, New York, 1929; THE AUTUMN OF LIFE from *EDGAR A. GUEST BROADCASTING*, copyright 1935, The Reilly & Lee Co. Used by permission. Our sincere thanks to the following whose addresses we were unable to locate: Marjorie Lindsey Brewer for THE PILGRIMS GIVE THANKS from *OUR AMERICAN HERITAGE*, copyright © 1958; Beulah Stoneman Douglas for MY HARVEST; Ruth Linnea Erickson for VESPER TIME from *HOMESPUN VERSE*, copyright © 1956 by Ruth Linnea Erickson; Stella Flowers Hastings for AFTER THE STORM from the *DAVIS' ANTHOLOGY OF NEWSPAPER VERSE For 1932* by Athie Sale Davis, copyright 1933 by Athie Sale Davis, originally published in *THE OAKLAND (Calif) TRIBUNE*; Starrlette L. Howard for GYPSY WIND; Harriet McKay for LINEAGE from the *DAVIS' ANTHOLOGY OF NEWSPAPER VERSE For 1934* by Athie Sale Davis, copyright 1935 by Athie Sale Davis, originally published in *THE PALM BEACH (Fla.) TIMES;* the Estate of Clinton B. Price for REFLECTIONS; Mary Clark Williams for FAMILY LOVE.